How to Write a Research Paper in 24 Hours

How to Write a Research Paper in 24 Hours

Roney McIntyre, Jr.

Acknowledgements

This book is dedicated to the people who've helped me with difficult subjects in school. It is also dedicated to the people who gave me their total trust and learned my methods to improve their writing level. It isn't easy trusting people these days, it seems as if everyone is trying to hustle someone.

How to Write a Research Paper in 24 Hours is very comprehensive, yet challenging. When you apply all these methods and see the improvements, you will wish someone taught you this several years ago. I remember my elementary school being ranked #1. I thank all of my teachers and coaches who gave their all to make sure we learned the fundamentals of English and thrive in writing.

ISBN-13: 978-1511605878
ISBN-10: 1511605871

Dedicated to those who love writing…
…People must begin to believe in writing again!

Table of Contents

How to Write a Research Paper in 24 Hours

Introduction
I.

There are tons of books out there claiming to be the best book to give tips and strategies on writing research papers. This book will not teach you proper English or grammar. This book will not teach you APA or MLA format. Those are things you should know at this point. If not, there are books and websites that would give you a thorough knowledge.

How to Write a Research Paper in 24 Hours will teach you just that. Many people will look at the title and conclude that such a feat is impossible. Those are the same people who cringe when the teacher or instructor says "A research paper will be required at the end of this course." The more you understand this book, the less time it will take you to complete any writing assignment.

Once structure and organization is mastered, creativity

will find its way in the heart of your research. How to Write a Research Paper in 24 Hours will show you how to control the data presented and keep it real towards your personal convictions. Writing from the heart with no solid academic citations will get you a failing grade; therefore you must master research to learn how to be true to your personal conviction and still manage to keep your work strictly academic.

The people who will succeed at this task are the people who believe they can do exactly what I say they can. At the end of this book, you will learn key skills and the framework needed to write a research paper in 24 hours. My job is to take the panic out of it. Once I break down how this is accomplished, 24 hours will seem like more than enough time.

Embracing your Creativity
II.

If done correctly and with respect to the original format of the assignment outlined by the teacher or the professor, there's sometimes plenty of room for creativity. Once creativity is discovered and embraced, the anxiety of doing well becomes a thing of the past. Most times the anxiety of writing a research paper comes from the added pressure knowing that the grade will make up most of the final grade.

To make matters worst, most teachers or professors only grammatically correct your rough draft and give you a few pointers. This would be awesome if you were working in a group and could combine the ideas of several people into the final paper. That isn't the case most of the time; all of the pressure is on single you to make a miracle out of something you're struggling with.

Embracing your creativity has the power to incorporate things you are passionate about into a topic or course you have very little interest in. For example, you may absolutely love poetry and spoken word. Given the excitement towards the craft, you may run across a piece from the era you're researching or a current work written about a person of the era you're writing about. You can add that poetry to your research paper and make it a little bit more interesting.

This is a good method to utilize, but do not overuse it. What I mean is do not find a piece of poetry that is several pages long just to meet the page requirements of the assignment. That foolish attempt will turn what could have been something creative into blatant disrespect to the teacher of professor. When using this method, make sure the poem is on topic and completely relative to what you're writing about.

Choking on the Pill of Rehabilitation:
The Pain, Price, and Placebo Exploitation of Substance Treatment for America's Juveniles

The Pain

America has created a back door for foolish decisions and has paved an escape route for irresponsible or manipulative people. America has created a victim culture, where criminal behavior or bad choices are passed on to others (Meadows, 2010, p. 39). America invests in the diagnosis, the treatment, and the exploitation. The victims are the pongs sliding through the social institutions and programs constructed by "the powers that be." Our culture is made up of many influences leading to temptations of the worst sort, especially for the emotionally insecure teen (Meadows, 2000, pg. 188). Linguist McWhorter (2005) says "Insecurity can make you just give up and while away your days in idle misery" (p. 167).

Deficits or imbalances in life (spirit, mind, body, social behavior, and environment) may lead individuals to seek out addictive behaviors as a way of fulfilling unmet needs (Duvall, Tindell, Oser, & Leukefeld, 2008, p. 1208). Public schools and universities confront a number of challenges, such as how to educate students and provide a safe learning environment for students and staff (Meadows, 2000, p. 175). Although only 4 percent of inner-city school students reported using hard drugs, 13 percent reported working for a drug dealer (Meadows, 2000, pgs. 175-176). Sociologist Edwin Lemert says that people engage in deviant behavior when they see themselves as "outsiders" and therefore attempt to live up to that label (Fuller, 2010, pp. 100-101).

The Price

8

At least one-quarter of the U.S. population will meet the criteria for a substance use disorder over the course of their lifetimes, making substance misuse the most common of all mental disorders (Hansell and Damour, 2006, p.2 56). According to Siegel (2009) "Each heroin addict is estimated to cost society more than $135,000.00 per year; an estimated half-million addicts cost society about $68 billion per year" (p. 66). Fuller (2010) also suggest that "This society simply cannot afford to spend the money and resources necessary to have a totally crime free society" (p. 28). In essence tax dollars are taken away from educational institutions and used to treat drug addicts rather than used to make tax payers safer through properly funded law enforcement.

The Placebo Effect of Exploitation

Since substance use is so ubiquitous, we must also look at the question of why people use drugs (Hansell and Damour, 2006, p. 257).The development of anomie is derived from Emile Durkheim's introduction of "deregulation," or normlessness. Durkheim later used the tern anomie to refer to a morally deregulated condition in which people have inadequate moral control over their behavior (Williams III and McShane, 2004, p. 96). Merton disagreed that changes and deregulation within society created anomie; instead, he felt that the critical ingredient was the control in the form of social norms (Williams III and McShane, 2004, p. 97). The shift in traditions and values creates social turmoil (Siegel, 2009, p. 175). From the two explanations it is safe to conclude that social norms and disruptions in life can influence criminal behavior, but the key to avoiding it is self-control.

With substance misuse, as with other disorders, the use of multiple components in explanations and treatments is the most helpful complete approach (Hansell and Damour, 2006, p. 289). Treatment doesn't work for every client every time, especially if our expectation is that one treatment exposure will eliminate the use of substance for the rest of the person's life (Hart, Ksir, & Ray, 2009, p. 441). Hart, Ksir, & Ray (2009) continue by explaining "There are no reliable "cures," and all of these conditions may require continuing care throughout the patient's life (p. 441). Given the often chronic nature of drug involvement among drug abusers in the justice system, treatment and other community services need to continue beyond the end of the sanction period (Anglin, Brown, Dembo, & Leukfeld, 2009, p. 94).

In Closing

The psychodynamic perspective on substance misuse was the first comprehensive psychological approach to addiction, and it is a foundation for many other contemporary psychological approaches (Hansell and Damour, 2006, p. 295). Multitudes of open-ended research and experimentation are a bit extreme and it is time to put this unnecessary study to rest. More efforts should be placed at the front end (before conception of a child) than at the back end (treatment and incarceration). The solution is to be responsible and take ownership of your decisions, not allowing victimhood to be an escape (McWhorter,

2005, p. 386).

<u>Writer's Remarks</u>

If you're trained in an environment of neglect, it is difficult to part from deviant coping mechanisms carried on well into your adulthood. Training a child to be sound morally gives him something to come back to when he matures and becomes lost in his folly. McWhorter 2000 says "The fact is that people will never all see the world the same way" (p. 314).

<u>McIntyre's Block Wall/ Elastic Band Theory</u>

Proverbs 22:6 says to "Train a child in the way he should go, and even when he is old he will not turn away from it." You can't whip a person back; they must come back after they've settled their rebellion in their spirit.

<u>Block Wall/Elastic Band Paradigm</u>

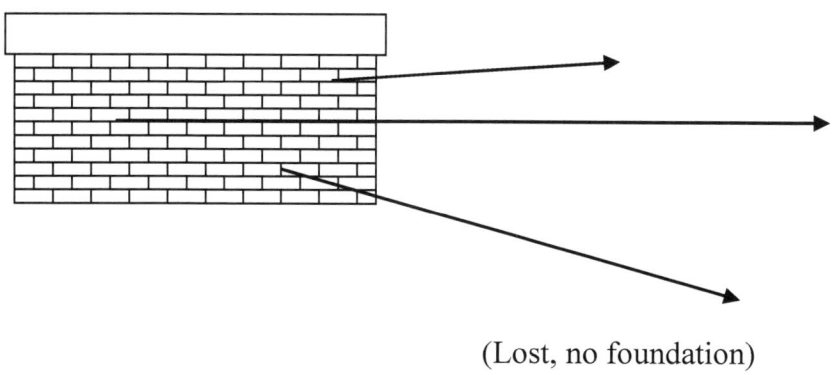

(Lost, no foundation)

11

Our job is to train a child in the right way. Parents shouldn't beat their selves up when the one they've raised chooses to go out in the deep end. No matter how far they go, the foundation has been set to come back to, as to not having one at all.

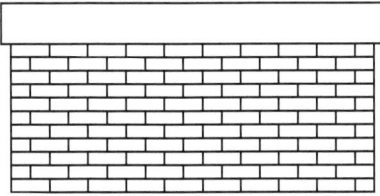

(Folkways and Morays)

Our streets might be safer by sweeping away what we consider to be riffraff, but other communities will have to deal with these human beings who feel alienated from society and are not bound to conventional behavior (Fuller, 2010, p. 232). Until America drops the nationality prefix, there will always be separation and discriminating distinctions instead of simply looking at everyone as human beings. Quick-fix rehabilitative efforts are nothing more than exploitation. Perfect order is achieved when home is in harmony. National oneness cannot be achieved if America itself is divided through labels, anti-intellectualism, and placebo pills of rehabilitation.

References

Anglin, M.D., Brown, B.S., Dembo, R., Leukfeld, C. (2009). Criminality and Addiction: Selected Issues for Future Policies, Practice, & Research. *Journal of Drug Issues,* 0022-0426/09/01 89-100.

Duvall, J.L, Tindell, M., Oser, C., Leukefeld, C. (2008). Persistence in Turning to Faith as a Predictor of Drug Use and Criminality Among Drug Court Clients. *Journal of Drug Issues,* 0022-0426/08/03 1207-1224.

Fuller, J.R. (2010). Criminal Justice: Mainstream and Crosscurrents 2nd Edition. Upper Saddle River, New Jersey: Prentice Hall.

Hansell, J., Damour, L. (2006). Abnormal Psychology. John Wiley & Sons, Inc.

Hart, C.L., Ksir, C., Ray, O. (2009). Drugs, Society, and Human Behavior 13th Edition. New York, New York: McGraw-Hill.

Meadows, R. J. (2000). Understanding Violence and Victimization 5th Edition. Upper Saddle River, New Jersey: Prentice Hall.

McWhorter, J. (2005). Winning the Race. Gotham Books.

Siegel, L.J. (2009). Criminology 10th Edition. Belmont, California: Thomson Wadsworth.

Williams III F.P., McShane M.D. (2004). Criminological Theory 4th Edition. Upper Saddle River, New Jersey: Pearson Prentice Hall.

Selecting Your Sources
III.

The previous paper showed a lot of creativity. Although it didn't use poetry or things of that nature, simple clip art was incorporated to give a visual of a common concept expressed in the Christian faith. As common as the saying is, I thought it would nice to have a visual of the concept and try to create a theory around it. Who knows, one day the theory may be further developed and widely used.

Another key element to writing quickly and effectively outside of creativity is selecting your sources. I find that many people spend days in the library finding books and materials online. At this point in time, I taught myself how to be in and out of the library in 15-30 minutes. Once you're done with this book, you will realize that's all you need.

Selecting your sources can be fun and creative as well. In the past, I found ways to incorporate poetry books I self-published into my paper. Instead of having a paper full of quotes from scholars, I found it very flattering to have a line or two out one of my works and cite my own name. Using this method, you can reference works written by family members. It gives a sense of pride when the completed work receives a very high grade in the end.

While selecting sources, always stay in line with what the instructor desires. If they say use only peer reviewed journal articles, don't submit them a paper with website articles and pages of poetry. In my opinion, only use website information to help better narrate what you're trying to explain in your paper. Those type of sources offer great details, but they aren't backed by reliable sources most of the time.

A good strategy I use when selecting journal articles is looking for articles I can use in more than one class. If I have one class in Juvenile Justice and another in Child Psychology, then I would look for an article along the lines of "Childhood Behavior that Leads to Criminality". This way I can use the article for both courses, reducing the research time for the opposite course. The same can be done with other formats of sources.

Introducing McIntyre's Victimization Revolution Theory:
"Psychology vs. Sociology Battle for Intellectual Hierarchy"

Open Wallet

The mental, physical, and social influential aspects of criminal behavior have been defined and debated since the early ages of criminology. The spiritual (an individual's sensitivity to life) has been denounced by esteemed intellectuals of the classical school of criminology (Fuller, 2010, p. 77). Systems and programs have been established to "treat" offenders and victims rather than prevent such misfortunes from occurring. There have been decades of enabling and manufacturing America's greatest commodity, "the victim."

America has become a nation of victims, where everyone is competing to be labeled as a victim (Meadows, 2010, p. 39). Over time, the definition of a victim has gone from being a defenseless creature to being senseless. In 1497, the definition of a victim was the sacrifice of a living creature. In 1660, the definition of a victim was a person who was hurt, tortured, or killed by another. By 1781, the definition of a victim became more sensitive, defining a victim as an individual that was being taken advantage of.

The current definition of a victim is a person who has been deceived or cheated by his or her own emotions or ignorance or by the dishonesty of others. A victim can also be created by some impersonal agency, such as a victim of misplaced confidence; swindling or optical illusion. By definition, if an individual is fooled by a magician's magic trick, that person is being victimized.

America has created a back door for foolish decisions and has paved an escape route for irresponsible and manipulative individuals. America has also created a "victim culture," where criminal behavior and bad choices are passed on to others (Meadows, 2010, p. 39). Meadows 2010 says "The victim culture interferes with helping those who truly need and deserve assistance" (p. 39).

The victim industry has been fueled by psychotherapists and outlines the direct economic and professional benefits that psychotherapists derive from perpetuating the idea of victimology (Meadows, 2010, p. 39). The assumptions of rationalism, the return of natural propensities, and a focus on early childhood allow the introduction of psychological and biological concepts into the explanation of criminality (Williams III and McShane, 2004, p. 313). Author Dineen discusses how therapists need patients, so they create disorders with which to label prospective customers (Meadows, 2010, p. 39). Are some capitalizing on victimization or are some people truly victims?

Powerful Social Institutions

According to Fuller (2010) "One of the methods used to determine guilt or innocence in earlier times was trial by ordeal, in which it was believed that God would intervene and save the innocent" (p. 76). In the Bible the rebellious guards told Jesus "If you are King, come down from the cross and save yourself!" The guards didn't say come down then they will believe Jesus is the Son of God. If Jesus had gotten down from the cross the guards would have said "Still not convinced. Now do this for me, and do that for me!" Similar to what the world is doing today.

The guards were in a sense exercising their freedom to criticize the powerful social institution known as

Christianity. The Enlightenment of the classical school of criminology advanced the scientific method in the physical sciences and allowed philosophers, playwrights, and novelist those same, but new at their time, freedom to criticize powerful social institutions (Fuller, 2010, p. 77). Over time the plain explanation of deviant behavior by the religious world became old news through the exciting theories (explanations) from the novelist, biologist, psychologist, and sociologist. As a result, the epic "psychology vs. sociology" battle to classify and treat victims has led to the biggest contribution along with the media in the Manufacturing of Victimization.

The Investment

Even those who are not directly affected by certain criminal behaviors directly are still affected through society' greatest tool, which is fear. Society's fear of crime is irrational. According to the fear-victimization paradox, the people who are less likely to be victimized (women and the elderly), are more fearful of crime than the most likely victims who statistically are young black males aged 18-24 (Meadows, 2010, pp. 4, 11). This irrational fear is a direct result of the horizontal transmission of knowledge. The gatekeepers of the airwaves and motion-pictures control and create aspects of this fear.

Berkley linguistics professor John McWhorter (2000) refers to Hollywood as having an "exploitative and oppressive nature" (p. 32). The media in its half-hearted interpretation of crime shares the same blame and nature. As irrational as the fear of victimization to women and the elderly actually is, the constant exploitation of fear by media makes it rational. Could social institutions be creating fear, disorders, and the treatment?

The Debt

Fueling the perception of police injustice is the media's quick reporting of police use of excessive force, particularly those cases involving minorities of disenfranchised persons living in low-income communities (Meadows, 2010, p. 205). According to Fuller (2010) "Given the decreasing crime rates of the last decade, it would seem that the media would present an improving picture of the crime situation in the United States" (pg. 33). As reflected in the media, the public seems to attribute criminal behavior to such things as drug use, a depressed economy, poor family life, and the influence of bad friends" (Williams III and McShane, 2004, p. 3). The media's half-hearted interpretation of crime in this sense fuels society's irrational perception of victimization. James Q. Wilson made this famous observation:

> Wicked people exist. Nothing avails except to set them apart from innocent people. And many people, neither wicked nor innocent, but watchful, dissembling, and calculating of their chances, ponder our reaction to wickedness as a clue to what they might profitably do (Siegel, 2009, p. 93).

Victims are those affected by wickedness, either intimate or done by exploiters for profit. The 14th Amendment says no state shall deprive any person of life, liberty, or property without due process of law (Fuller,

2010, p. 216). Shouldn't it be illegal to rob a person of their mind and sense of well-being in efforts to continue profiting off of victimization? America invests in the diagnosis, the treatment, and the exploitation. The victims are the pongs sliding through the social institutions and programs constructed by "the powers that be."

Credibility

The solution to victimization isn't more and more theories, the solution is sticking to one. Systems and programs have been set up to "treat" offenders and victims rather than prevent such misfortunes from occurring. The problem with addressing the core cause of criminality is that it will eliminate entire social institutions and practices, thus ending the highly supported battle for hierarchy in intellectual relevance.

Charles Goring did the best job of capturing the reality of victimization. In 1913 Goring published The English Convict, which was the result of a study of 3,000 convicts. The study revealed that there was only a little difference between the physical characteristics of criminals and non-criminals. In this study Goring found significant relationship between crime and what he referred to as defective intelligence, which involves traits such as feeblemindedness, epilepsy, insanity, and defective social instinct. This idea gave birth to the Cognitive theory.

Goring believed that criminal behavior was inherited and could be controlled by limiting the reproduction of families who produced mentally defective children (Siegel, 2009, pp. 136-137). Limiting reproduction is impossible in today's society where sex is the biggest marketing tool. Victimization occurs before conception of a child. What are happening today are criminals making criminals and the media exploiting their criminal personality.

In 1976 Samuel Yochelson and Stanton Samenow reintroduced the case for criminal personality in a case study involving between 230 and 270 inmates at St. Elizabeth's Hospital for the criminally insane in Washington, D.C. (Williams III and McShane, 2004, p. 44). Yochelson and Samenow pronounced that the causes of crime are not social, economic, or psychological inner-conflicts. Instead, they claimed that all criminals are born with abnormal thinking patterns that affect their ability to make decisions (Williams III and McShane, 2004, p. 44-45). Yochelson and Samenow claimed to have found fifty-two different criminal thinking patterns. The theoretical position that all criminals have different thinking patterns was popular in federal government circles for a while (Williams III and McShane, 2004, p. 45).

According to Williams III and McShane (2004) "Psychological perspectives have found much more favor with policymakers as a standard approach to criminal behavior." (p. 47). Sociological versions of positivist theory have been the cornerstone of many of our crime policies for the past thirty years (Williams III and McShane, 2004, p. 47). According to Williams III and McShane (2004):

Cognitive theory dwells on the differences in thinking patterns between "normal" and criminal individuals, thus contributing to the assumption that criminal behavior is a result of some thinking failure of the individual. This has been translated into "bad people

23

bring on their own bad behavior and simply deserve to be punished for their own decisions." In short, policymakers see punishment as the way to impress on bad individuals that their thinking needs correcting; no treatment programs are needed. Psychologists, however, have generally not subscribed to the no-treatment philosophy and have created techniques designed to teach offenders how to think rationally and realistically (p. 47).

It is possible to train an adult to do a task, but it is impossible to train an adult morally. By the age of 13, most children have chosen their paths and ways of reasoning. If you're trained in an environment of neglect, it is difficult to part from deviant coping mechanisms carried on well into your adulthood. Training a child to be sound morally gives him something to come back to when he matures and becomes lost in his folly.

Closed Wallet

Political and religious factions claim to speak for the "silent majority," an ostensibly large group of strongly religious, conservative citizens (Williams III and McShane, 2004, p. 308). These same citizens are the victims of exploitation, giving policymakers and the media control over their spirit. Berkley linguistics professor John McWhorter (2000) says "Victimology, Separatism, and Anti-intellectualism are not mere fringe phenomena local to disaffected inner-city residents and certain colorful powermongers" (p. 185). Such misleading perspectives distract attention from potentially effective solutions while rendering seductive other solutions that in fact only perpetuate the problem they address (McWhorter, 2000, p. 185). The question remains who are the true victims?

The tax-payers are the victims. The great men and women who put their lives on the line are the victims. The students who look át the drug dealers as the problem are the victims. The proud student standing at "the mountain top" sensing a false ideology of achievement is the victim. The great men and women who go unnoticed are the victims. These people are the victim of the widespread disease known as Victimology (McWhorter, 2000, p. 29).

The only victims are the special victims which are those truly victimized as related to the origin of the definition of a victim, the defenseless person who is hurt, tortured, or killed by another. The soft definition of a victim opens the door for abuse and false accusations with the motive to provide an alibi, seek revenge, and obtain sympathy and attention to cope with personal and social stress situations (Meadows, 2010, p. 39). According to McWhorter (2000) "Only a fraction of our population are victims in any meaningful sense" (p. 220).

Americans are told that they are traumatized, victimized, and are in need of a psychotherapist or personal injury attorney. Those who do not feel victimized may be labeled as being in denial. In other words, if you do not feel you're a victim we'll convince you that you are (Meadows, 2010, p. 39). The solution is to be responsible and take ownership of your decisions, not allowing victimhood to be an escape (McWhorter, 2005, p. 386).

References

Dictionary.com

Fuller, J.R. (2010). Criminal Justice: Mainstream and Crosscurrents 2nd Edition. Upper Saddle River, New Jersey: Prentice Hall.

McWhorter, J. (2000). Losing the Race. New York, New York: Harper Perennial.

McWhorter, J. (2005). Winning the Race. Gotham Books.

Meadows, R. J. (2010). Understanding Violence and Victimization 5th Edition. Upper Saddle River, New Jersey: Prentice Hall.

Siegel, L.J. (2009). Criminology 10th Edition. Belmont, California: Thomson Wadsworth.

Williams III F.P., McShane M.D. (2004) Criminological Theory 4th Edition. Upper Saddle River, New Jersey: Pearson Prentice Hall.

Structure and Organization
IV.

While thoroughly examining the text required for my criminal justice courses, I saw a battle going on within it. Being that I haven't heard much discussion of this battle, I created a theory around it. Maybe this too can be developed and accepted worldwide. Only time will tell. Nevertheless, it adds to all the methods and strategies discussed this far. What better sources than the books assigned to the major you're studying?

The problem students make with citing from books assigned to the course, they make the mistake of copying and using common knowledge. An example would be:

"My paper is on Criminology. Criminology is the study of... Criminology was founded by... The book says..." All of which is wrong and unnecessary. While digging deep, I found a battle going on between sociologists and psychologists and explained it in a way that isn't taught. You too can do this, then use sources to expound on your findings.

Structure and organization is very important when trying to reduce the time spent on doing research papers. While looking at the 2 sample papers thus far, look at the subtitles that are underlined and how they guide the reader when the focus of the information changes. Again, if an instructor says to not use them, don't use them. As I said before, if done respectfully, most instructors won't mind the added touches.

A method I use is putting all the cited material in one document. This helps with organization. I then arrange the information in a flow that makes sense and drives home the point I am trying to prove. Once everything is organized, you can think of clever subtitles to give the paper structure. Once this is done, the remainder of your time is simply used tying the ideas together and writing transitional sentences into the next set of ideas within the paper.

The Future of the Criminal Justice System Beyond the Victimization Revolution

Beyond Deliberate Victimization

Meadows (2010) says that "The operation of the criminal justice system and decisions by its agents, however, sometimes create victims inadvertently or deliberately through its vast discretionary process" (p. 204). The question that leads to the solution would be to ask oneself who are the people most discriminated against in the discretionary process? It has been reported that members of racial, ethnic, and other minorities of vulnerable groups often face harassment, arbitrary detention, and abusive treatment by law enforcement apparatus and disparate treatment by prosecutors and the courts (Meadows, 2010, p. 204). Could this deliberate victimization of minorities be the cause of the statistic suggesting that the criminals are young black males aged 18-24?

According to the 2006 UCR statistics, over half of the incidents with bias motivation are due to race. Anti-black and anti-white offenses lead the category with 3 times as many black victims of this occurrence than white. Therefore statistically black youths are more likely to be victims of crime and victims of bias (race) motivation. Meadows (2010) argues that

"Fueling the perception of police injustice is the media's quick reporting of police use of excessive force, particularly those cases involving minorities of disenfranchised persons living in low-income communities" (p. 205). Doesn't the deliberate victimization of these minorities and the failure to mention that minorities are 3 times more likely to be victims of hate crimes than whites when giving the statistics of crime justify the attention given to the injustice?

Berkley linguistics professor John McWhorter (2000) says "Victimology, Separatism, and Anti-intellectualism are not mere fringe phenomena local to disaffected inner-city residents and certain colorful powermongers" (p. 185). Such misleading perspectives distract attention from potentially effective solutions while rendering seductive other solutions that in fact only perpetuate the problem they address (McWhorter, 2000, p. 185). To go beyond the labeling and future manufacturing of victims, Americans must get past race and truly strive to resolve crime instead of continuing to exploit criminality for profitable gain. Although the media and other powerful social institutions have made fortunes from exploiting deliberate victimization, the solution isn't in their hands.

The Roots of Deliberate Victimization

The political nature of the Chicago police in the early 20th century resulted in a system in which the police took bribes, solicited votes, harassed the homeless, beat suspects, and assisted gamblers (Fuller, 2010, p. 159). According to Meadows (2010) "There is no monetary relief, only injunctive relief, such as orders to end the misconduct and changes in the agency's policies and procedures that resulted in or allow the misconduct" (p. 208). In 1954 the Supreme Court made segregation unlawful on paper, although the orders were given, police and attack dogs were at schools prohibiting black people from entering. Orders to resolve a moral or ethical issue is meaningless when the hearts of those upholding the law are hardened. One aspect of the solution to criminality is, and always has been getting people to see past class, ethnicity, and low-income communities.

Following the Civil Rights movement, the criminal justice system took its first steps in changing its attitude to minorities as a whole. During the 1950s and 1960s, a progressive attitude in correctional circles advocated rehabilitation over punishment, and the indeterminate sentence enjoyed wide popularity (Fuller, 2010, p. 347). Williams III and McShane (2004) explained "Since the early 1970s, society has been moving in a decidedly conservative direction" (p. 308). The discipline of criminal justice expanded throughout the 1970s also, roughly 3 years after the 1967 President's Commission in Law Enforcement and the Administration of Justice (Williams III and McShane, 2004, p. 310).

The most damaging victimization occurs when the justice system victimizes citizens through its accusatory or decision-making process, as when a person is wrongfully charged, convicted, imprisoned, or punished (Meadows, 2010, p. 209). The lack of funds to hire more police to patrol high-crime areas or more probation and parole officers to supervise offenders contributes to inadvertent victimization (Meadows, 2010, p. 204). Where is all the money going?

The Weeds

The weeds of the criminal justice system are the illegal drug epidemic, "vanishing" resources, and other financial squandering practiced within the criminal justice system. When people consider the disparities between how street crime and corporate crimes are dealt with by the criminal justice system, one can begin to appreciate why critical criminologists continue the tradition of studying Marx and considering the role of social class and power in society (Fuller, 2010, p. 104). Policymakers and law enforcement singles out poor communities by spending more money to police them, all the while turning a blind eye to white collar crime. According to Fuller (2010) "One need only look at how political campaigns are financed to see how big money influences the making of laws" (p. 103). It seems as if more money is spent to create the laws than to hire people to enforce them. Why is that?

According to Siegel (2009) "Each heroin addict is estimated to cost society more than $135,000.00 per year; an estimated half-million addicts cost society about $68 billion per year" (p. 66). Tax payer's tax dollars are divided between healthcare, national defenses, education, highways, law enforcement, and other legitimate services. Fuller (2010) predicts that "The criminal justice system, by some estimates, could bankrupt the nation if funded for all its legitimate needs" (p. 28). Fuller (2010) also suggest that "This society simply cannot afford to spend the money and resources necessary to have a totally crime free society" (p. 28). In essence, tax dollars are taken away from educational institutions and used to treat drug addicts rather than used to make tax payers safer through properly funded law enforcement systems.

Walls of Silence

Many victims feel anger when they see defendants enjoying due-process rights while their voices remain unheard (Fuller, 2010, p. 315). Inadvertent victimization fuels the breeding ground for blood feuds. The combination of political neglect along with deliberate victimization leads to the suffering of strain theory by minorities in high crime areas. The fear of retaliation from an enemy contributes to The Street Code of Silence (G-code); the fear of isolation within the police sub-culture of law enforcement contributes to the Blue Wall of Silence.

Society has to be careful how it isolates people. Sociologist Edwin Lemert says that people engage in deviant behavior when they see themselves as "outsiders" and therefore attempt to live up to that label (Fuller, 2010, pp. 100-101). According to Siegel (2010) Wilson and Kelling conclude:

Just as physicians now recognize the importance of fostering health rather than simply treating illness, so the police and the rest of society ought to recognize the importance of maintaining intact communities without broken windows (p. 498).

Open Windows of Hope in the Criminal Justice System

Retribution is an ancient motive with religious connotations, and for many people it is one of the most important goals of the criminal justice system (Fuller, 2010, p. 30). The debate as to whether rehabilitation works and whether the criminal justice system allocates suitable resources toward this goal is ongoing (Fuller, 2010, p. 30). Victimization Revolution Theory shines a light on deliberate victimization caused by powerful social institution in efforts of profitable gain.

McIntyre's solution to criminal behavior is illustrated in the Soul Restoration Paradigm (will not be displayed in this book). McIntyre's Soul Restoration Theory is based on the idea that idleness leads to idolatry. McIntyre believes that self-will isn't enough when a person has slipped into darkness and really wants to be rehabilitated thereafter. The soul (sensitivity to life) can only be tapped into by the sincere sensitivity, unconditional love, and commitment of another person. Therefore the solution to criminal behavior and the future of the criminal justice is in the hands-on reconstruction of the "silent majority."

References

Dictionary.com

Fuller, J.R. (2010). Criminal Justice: Mainstream and Crosscurrents 2nd Edition. Upper Saddle River, New Jersey: Prentice Hall.

McWhorter, J. (2000). Losing the Race. New York, New York: Harper Perennial.

Meadows, R. J. (2010). Understanding Violence and Victimization 5th Edition. Upper Saddle River, New Jersey: Prentice Hall.

Miller, Roger L., Gaines L. K. (2007). Criminal Justice in Action 4th Edition. Belmont, CA: Thomson Wadsworth.

Siegel, L.J. (2009). Criminology 10th Edition. Belmont, California: Thomson Wadsworth.

Williams III F.P., McShane M.D. (2004). Criminological Theory 4th Edition. Upper Saddle River, New Jersey: Pearson Prentice Hall.

Taking it to the Next Level
V.

You should have noticed that the paper you just read was a continuation of the one that went before it. Most of the same sources were used, but this time new ones were added to give the paper more substance. It took a theory I created and applied it to the future of the criminal justice system. This was also a good example of taking a research paper to the next level.

Taking a research paper to the next level is simply going from explaining to your instructor what he or she may already know to creating concepts that are completely original. In doing so, you can create a body of work that can follow you throughout your entire educational experience. What is too early to think about your master thesis? What is too early to think about your dissertation? Even if your body of work don't hold up to the expectations of future instructors, at least you didn't go into their course unprepared.

One key source to taking your research to the next level is attentively listening to your instructor. Once you get into the habit of doing this as strategy, you will learn all of the important keys to making the highest grade possible directly through them. Instructors recommend books all the time, it would be a good idea to buy all of them and use them as sources when the material applies to the topic you are writing about.

Another way to take your research to the next level is finding out what books or articles your instructor has published. This will also show the instructor that you are paying attention. We all know that some courses require you to conduct real time interviews with people in your field of study. Taking your research paper to the next level involves incorporating these types of things without being instructed to. Simply put, taking it to the next level is going that extra mile.

Slaves of the Master:
The Future of Newjacks and Inmates in the Corrections Industry

---

Introduction

Studies have shown that most of the new inmates swelling the system are nonviolent drug offenders subject to mandatory sentencing laws (Conover, 2000, p. 232). Allen Latessa & Ponder (2010) project that "By the year 2012, prison population will have grown to approximately 1.8 million Americans" (p. 199). According to Conover (2010) "Documentary films (such as the excellent The Farm), tend to focus on inmate life. He continues "But prison, it occurred to me, is actually a world of two sides- two colors of uniform- the "us" and the "them" (p. 18). Looking at a dying economy along with a growing prison population, what is the immediate future of new correctional officers?

Officer after officer will tell you there's no way in hell you'd want your kid to be a CO (Conover, 2000, p. 21). Given this statement, it is reasonable to ask why this is so. Open discussions at a community college in New Orleans revealed the lackadaisical attitude of correctional administration and the insulting wage and salaries. Salaries are on the decline while prison population is on the incline. McIntyre will provide a look into the future of ("us") Newjacks beginning with the attitudes of Angola inmates ("them") in The Farm documentary.

"Them"

An Angola correctional officer concluded his interview in the "The Farm" documentary expressing, "It's sad what we see." Inmate John Brown's last words before his resting bed in Point Lookout were, "Wow." Geriatric patient Bones' last words of wisdom before his trip to the same place were, "It's not where you go, its how you go." The thing each person had in common was a personalized sense of hope and a heightened perspective of moral responsibility and accountability.

You can't erase the past, but you can make corrections (McIntyre, 2008, p. 32). A philosophy exploited by the growth industry and privatization. Their practice exploits the inmates' transitional period while using them as an in-cage scientific experiment evaluating a man's breaking point on his road to efficacy. Can a caged bird fly? A better question explaining the methods of corrections is, "Can we make a caged bird believe he can fly in efforts to reduce riots and hopelessness within correctional facilities?"

The Cost

The death penalty has cost taxpayers $25.3 million dollars since 1983 (Allen, Latessa & Ponder, 2010, p. 279). Taxpayers are also paying $3.3 billion dollars for medical care for inmates. Tax payers are paying up to $200,000 per bed in prisons. We live in a country that put more investment in the cure at the back-end after the criminal is created than the front-end when it's in the making.

The Unnecessary Panel

Death row inmate John Brown confessed to having a better concern for his life and others after being incarcerated. In a sermon, inmate Bishop Tannehill said, "Prison rescued me." These prisoners are conditioned like many others to plead to a panel of board members who only hear the hardened hearts of the victims. If the outcry of an openly racist "victim" is enough to not even consider the validity of crucial evidence, why is the board even there?

"Us"

Certainly, the lack of adequate personnel is a crucial factor (Allen, Latessa & Ponder, 2010, p. 184). "The immediate requirement is not an influx of professional staff, but extensive training aimed at the habitual work patterns of uninterested, politically appointed, and unqualified jail personnel" (Allen, Latessa & Ponder, 2010, p. 185). This all goes back to responsibility and accountability. The future of corrections isn't a new-generational jail. The future of correctional systems is a new generation of professional staff minus the smoke and mirrors of meaningless boards, ineffective treatment, and social experimentation.

The Future of Newjacks and Inmates

Though the rate of violent crime in the country is down 20 percent since 1991, the number of people in prison or jail has risen by 50 percent (Conover, 2000, p. 232). There has to be a change in the attitudes of "the powers that be" if America is to grow and reconstruct vital systems governing the safety of society. Rick Kingsley called his career a life sentence in eight-hour shifts (Conover, 2000, p. 21).

Thomas Matt Osborne made this observation:

I believe every man in this place hates and detests the system under which he lives. He hates it even when he gets along without friction. He hates it even when he knows it is bad; for it tends to crush slowly but irresistibly the good in himself (Conover, 2000, p. 197).

The hope and mental well-being of both the inmates and COs are being compromised and exploited. We have a system that creates work opportunities within the institution for the inmates while compromising the salaries of the people putting their lives on the line to oversee these inmates. It is similar to the war veterans being denied benefits or the police officer injured on duty now begging for financial assistance. The treatment advocates will argue the side of the prisoner when given these analyses. The clearest reality of inmates was given by Jack Henry Abbott in this observation:

... A man is taken away from his experience of society, taken away from the experience

of a living planet of living things, when he is sent to prison.

A man is taken away from other prisoners, from his experience of other people,

when he is locked away in solitary confinement in the hole.

Every step of the way removes him from experience and narrows it down to only

the experience of himself...

The *concept* of death is simple: it is when a living thing no longer

entertains experience.

So when a man is taken farther and farther away from experience, he is being taken

     to his death (Conover, 2000, p. 126).

Ted Conover ended his book quoting an inmate indirectly describing Malcolm X's "house Negro and the field Negro." He expressed how the house Negro was sad when the house burned down as to the field Negro being happy to see the house burning down. Conover (2000) said "I only wondered how bad things would have to get before he could see it burning down with himself inside" (p. 309). Roney McIntyre, Jr. believes that house is burning down with the inmates; the COs, the economy, and all those who are suffering that have put their lives on the line for the well-being of American citizens. Bureaucrats at the mercy of paperwork must come from behind their desk and stand up for the people at the mercy of moral obligation and economical degradation.

The Conclusion

Responsibility and accountability must echo throughout the prisons and every social institution in the United States of America. "Only when American society decides which ideology or combination of ideologies most deserves its support will the problems facing the correctional administrator be properly addressed" (Allen, Latessa & Ponder, 2010, p. 54). Whether guarding Sing Sing or farming Angola, the total well-being of the correctional institution should come before paperwork and prison growth. Exploiting hopes to inmates over a period of life is not only costly to taxpayers but is no more humane than lynching them and eliminating hope immediately. "The conservative movement in the political arena continues to cause a steady move to the right in corrections, wreaking havoc with the shrinking efforts at rehabilitation, which works. The turmoil continues" (Allen, Latessa & Ponder, 2010, p. 35).

References

Allen, H. E., Latessa, E. J., Ponder, B. S. (2010). Corrections in America an Introduction 12th edition. Upper Saddle River, NJ: Pearson Prentice Hall.

Conover, Ted. (2000). New Jack: Guarding Sing Sing. New York: Random House.

Transitioning from Student to Expert
VI.

The previous paper only used 2 sources. The two sources were the textbook and the required novel. The paper was based off of a documentary we watched. This shows that a paper can be thorough despite having only a limited amount of sources. Whether its 2 sources or 20, knowing how to use them effectively will make you transition from student to expert.

What makes a person an expert is the ability to be a one-stop-shop for information or a skill to be rendered. This transition as it relates to research papers requires time and practice. With time and practice, you master structure as it relates to format and organizing your information. The student hopes for a high passing grade. The expert knows he or she will receive the highest grade possible.

The person who considers themselves an expert doesn't

mind playing the role of student. The expert will sit in a class and ask the same questions the student hoping to pass will ask. The expert sees the value of one on one time with the instructor, basically showing humility. Outside of consecutive A's on every writing assignment, you will not be able to tell the expert from the person who feels they're just a student. There's absolutely no reward or merit letting people know you have an advantage in writing.

As you transition from student to expert, know that expert in this case is just a metaphor for understanding all the methods and techniques given in this book. No matter how much you think you know, everyone from the student to the president of the educational institution, has something of value they can add to your pool of knowledge. Make the transition, but keep it quiet.

Society of Saints?
"Saving Our Sons For Real":
Deconstructing Walls and Codes of Silence, Reconstructing Pipelines of Communication Between Police Officers and Delinquents

Colors

"As students today, young black people are walking against the wind" (McWhorter, 2000, p. 161). "When a race is disparaged and disenfranchised for centuries and then abruptly given freedom, a ravaged racial self-image makes victimology and separatism natural developments" (McWhorter, 2000, p. 162). "A failure to rectify social conditions, if they are also important, will simply make matters worse and over the long term will cost much more in increased crime, suffering, and deterioration of neighborhoods" (William III and McShane, 2004, p. 24)."Crime has attractiveness to those with propensities toward it, thus the crime-propensity affinity entices individuals and promises pleasure" (William III and McShane, 2004, p. 276). Is this group of individuals coerced into criminality in efforts to increase crime and create a target for law enforcement?

Communication

"The application and enforcement of law leads to a focus on the behavior of less powerful group, thus disproportionately "criminalizing" the members of those groups" (William III and McShane, 2004, p. 179). "According to the thought of the Classical School, the criminal justice system should respect the rights of all people" (Williams & McShane, 2004, p. 19). "Although the poor know the right thing to be done, they lack the skill to deal with government double talk in laying out plans" (Scheibla, 1968, p. 131). "Since law embodies the values of those who create it, law is more likely to criminalize the actions if those outside the power group" (William III and McShane, 2004, p. 168). Which group does the police officer speak for, if they speak for any at all?

Broken Channels of Communication

"The code of silence, often referred to as the "blue curtain" or "blue veil", is the tendency of the law enforcement personnel to not share information with others" (Dempsey and Forst, 2012, p. 218)."It is basically a non-written rule that you do not roll over, tell on your partner, your companion" (Dempsey and Forst, 2012, p. 154). Those same codes of silence in law enforcement are parallel to the street code (G-Code), understood as the "no snitching" rule. If criminality within law enforcement is kept hidden, how can channels of communication between the police and the community be established?

"The belief is that others outside the police profession couldn't possibly understand the challenges that officers face is absorbed early in the training and socialization process of the job" (Dempsey and Forst, 2012, p. 218). "Police wisdom has on a wide scale overridden the legislative unwisdom embodied in the literal terms of the full enforcement legislation" (Fuller, 2010, p. 204). "The agents of law, in the enforcement efforts, perpetuate the values embodied in law and thus help keep in power those who already have power" (William III and McShane, 2004, p. 168). "Law itself represents a resource" (William III and McShane, 2004, p. 168). "Indeed, with the mistrust of government growing during the late 1960s and early 1970s, labeling was one way to critique and explain the abuses of power" (William III and McShane, 2004, p. 168).

Roots to the Abortion of Justice

"At the end of the 1950s society was becoming conscious of racial inequality, segregation, and civil rights" (William III and McShane, 2004, p. 141). "While the nation still was reeling from the shock of President Kennedy's assassination, Lyndon Johnson started work on the War on Poverty the day after he became President. He called it "My kind of program"" (Scheibla, 1968, p. 9). "Many members of Congress were not surprised when they saw the War on Poverty lose battle after battle. They had known it was a fraud from the beginning and voted for it only because politicians who want to stay in office don't usually oppose doling out federal funds to their constituents" (Scheibla, 1968, p. 249).

Head Start to Poverty and Broken Homes

In 1966, Eugene Hill from the Center for Community Action Services in Albuquerque made this evaluation: If a man is unemployed, a child day-care nursery doesn't solve his problem… You prescribe an asprin for my cancer and give it to my child" (Scheibla, 1968, p. 184).

In the spring of 1967, the Knoxville News Sentinel sagely commented "Any man who thinks he is going to be happy and prosperous by letting the government take care of him should take a close look at the American Indian" (Scheibla, 1968, p. 252).

"Any social environment contains several possible situations, each of which might provide different cues and consequences for a behavior" (William III and McShane, 2004, p. 220). "Many lower-class males are raised in fatherless households. Learning behavior and attitudes appropriate to adult male roles thus poses special problems" (William III and McShane, 2004, p. 127). Who do we blame; underemployed fathers, absent fathers, the government, or the police?

"African American sociologist E Franklin Frazier suggested that "Black adolescent boys learn criminology from older peers or family members and begin patterns of delinquent behavior around eleven or twelve years of age" (William III and McShane, 2004, p. 61). "Through watching, or otherwise knowing about an individual receiving punishment for committing an offense, others would learn that such behavior is not profitable and thus would not commit similar acts" (William III and McShane, 2004, p. 18). "We learn values from important people around us. Those values either support or oppose criminal behavior" (William III and McShane, 2004, p. 87). "More recently, social control theories have led to renewed emphasis on the importance of school and family in the fight against crime" (William III and McShane, 2004, p. 47).

Education?

James Baldwin said, "Education is a billion dollar industry, and the least important part of the industry is the child. I think this is criminal, but this is the way it works."

Dempsey & Forst (2012) suggested "A society will always have a certain number of deviants and deviance is really a normal phenomenon. Any society without crime and deviance is, by definition, abnormal" (p. 195). "Crime and delinquency are transmitted by frequent contact with criminal traditions that have developed over time in disorganized areas of the city" (William III and McShane, 2004, p. 67). Could powerful social institutions in society be subconsciously manufacturing delinquency in black communities and creating a class of delinquents for exploitation?

Catch, Profit, and Release?

"The prison cannot fail to produce delinquents" (Foucault, 1995, p. 266). "It does so by the very type of existence it imposes on its inmates; the prison should educate its inmates, but can a system of education addressed to a man reasonably have as its object to act against the wishes of nature" (Foucault, 1995, p. 266)? "Police surveillance provides the prison with offenders, which the prison transforms into delinquents, the targets and auxiliaries of police supervisions, which regularly send back a certain number of them to prison" (Foucault, 1995, p. 282). Knowing the misappropriation of funds committed to street crime as to white collar crime, it is safe to conclude that the eyes of the law are pinned on a certain group of disenfranchised black males.

Lethal Injection

"Victimology today pulses through the very

bloodstream of African American identity" (McWhorter, 2000, p. 49). "The most damning way in which separatism forces black Americans into self-sabotage is in identifying cultural blackness with pardoning and even glorifying immoral behavior" (McWhorter, 2000, p. 81). "The fact is that we will never all see the world the same way" (William III and McShane, 2004, p. 314). How do we (police, policy makers, fathers, educators, leaders) remove the damaging tint called anti-intellectualism from our minds long enough to see delinquents as humans?

The Public Execution

"The public execution is to be understood not only as a judicial, but also as a political ritual" (Foucault, 1995, p. 47). Beccaria argued "If the state can take a life, where is the profit in allowing the state to govern us" (William III and McShane, 2004, p. 20)? "Discipline sometimes requires enclosure, the specification of a place heterogeneous to all others and closed in upon itself" (Foucault, 1995, p. 141). Although executions are private, aren't people being executed through the media by projecting someone's opinion before the due process of law is carried out?

The Burial

James Baldwin made this observation:
> Brother has murdered brother knowing it was his brother. White men have lynched Negroes knowing to be their sons. White women have burned Negroes knowing to be their lovers. It is not a racial problem.

55

It's a problem whether or not you're willing to look at your life and be responsible for it, and then begin to change it.

"We must neither behave as children by resisting honesty, nor allow ourselves to be treated as children by having honesty withheld" (McWhorter, 2000, p. 151). There are no efforts of policing that can truly save our sons. Remove the federal billions of dollars from ineffective programs and create jobs that a young man can earn a salary sufficient enough to support his family, not minimum wage. That is grounds for failure. As educators, if we're going to tell receptive ears that crime is done by black males 16-24, we must take that same energy and report that blacks are 3 times victims of bias (hate) crimes than every other race.

Colors of the Wind, a Criminal Justice Student's Interpretation;

You think I'm just an ignorant savage   (delinquent)
And you've been so many places; I guess it must be so
But still I cannot see, if the savage one is me
How can there be so much that you don't know?
You don't know...

You think you own whatever land you land on
                                (black community)
The earth is just a dead thing you can claim
                                (human rights)
But I know every rock and tree and creature
                                (lower class)
Has a life, has a spirit, has a name.
                                (human)

You think the only people who are people
Are the people who look and think like you
But if you walk the footsteps of a stranger
You'll learn things you never knew you never knew

Have you ever heard the wolf cry to the blue corn moon
                              (our pains are similar and different)
Or asked the grinning bobcat why he grinned
                              (we share the same smiles)
Can you sing with all the voices of the mountain
                              (communication on all levels)
Can you paint with all the colors of the wind?
                              (races)
Can you paint with all the colors of the wind?
                              (young black males)

Come run the hidden pine trails of the forest
                              (ghetto)
Come taste the sun-sweet berries of the earth
                              (soul food)
Come roll in all the riches all around you
                              (the free things in life)
And for once never wonder what they're worth
                              (exploitation)
The rainstorm and the river are my brothers
                              ("criminals")
The heron and the otter are my friends
                              (victims of drug dependency)
And we are all connected to each other
                              (human)
In a circle in a loop that never ends
                              (circle of life)

Have you ever heard the wolf cry to the blue corn moon
                              (pray to God for help)
Or let the eagle tell you where he's been
                                   (experience)
Can you sing with all the voices of the mountain
                                  (love everyone)
Can you paint with all the colors of the wind?
                                      (all races)
Can you paint with all the colors of the wind?
                          (especially the neglected)

How high does a sycamore grow?
                           (hope/ glass ceiling)
If you cut it down then you'll never know
                                   (sensitivity)
And you'll never hear the wolf cry to the blue corn moon
                                 (communication)
For whether we are white or copper skinned
                                (black and white)
We need to sing with all the voices of the mountain
                                          (love)
We need to paint with all the colors of the wind

You can own the earth and still
                             (Death and Money)
All you'll own is earth until
                                 (privatization)
You can paint with all the colors of the wind

Criminal Justice Strategy
Saving Our Sons For Real Plan of Action

A prominent New Orleans public figure said "We must be willing to do what is difficult for the sake of doing what is right." It is common to hear someone suggest that educating delinquents is in turn making smarter criminals. It is the fear of encountering well educated, white collar people that make law enforcement more comfortable with targeting young black males. An educated individual (black or white) knows the law and will challenge the commonly uneducated police officer; the educated individual is often connected to someone who's on the "we don't want to cross this person" list.

To save our sons for real, we must value education and look at everyone as humans. We must plug the pipeline to prison by opening channels of communication between law enforcement personnel and the community. It is time for men to stand up in struggling communities and aid our police officers instead of demonizing them through senseless, unsupported rhetoric. We must abort separatist terms such as racism and sexism, and substitute them with the over-arching ideology known as anti-intellectualism. In time, in effort, and in justice, we will become a Society of Saints.

"Violence is not Inevitable"

References

Dempsey, J.S., Forst, L.S. (2012). An Introduction to Policing 6th Edition. Clifton Park, NY: Delmar.

Disney - Colors of the Wind Lyrics Album: Pocahontas http://www.stlyrics.com/songs/d/disney6472/colorsofthewind512086.html

Foucault, M. (1995). Discipline & Punishment, The Birth of the Prison. New York, NY: Vintage Books.

Fuller, J.R. (2010). Criminal Justice: Mainstream and Crosscurrents 2nd Edition. Upper Saddle River, New Jersey: Prentice Hall.

McWhorter, J. (2000). Losing the Race: Self-Sabotage in Black America. New York, NY: The Free Press.

Scheibla, S. (1968). Poverty Is Where the Money Is. New Rochelle, New York: Arlington House.

Williams III, F.P., McShane, M.D. (2004). Criminological Theory 4th Edition. Upper Saddle River, New Jersey: Pearson Prentice Hall.

How to Write a Research Paper in 24 Hours
VII.

The previous paper is a combination of all the methods and techniques discussed in this book. The idea was inspired by a stop the violence initiative led by the Mayor of New Orleans in 2011 called "Saving Our Sons". What you just read is a combination of many ideas talked about and written about during my two years studying criminal justice. Ideas were taken to the next level by using recent sources and sources dating back to the 1960s. One of the secrets to future success is incorporating all things learned into your final projects.

Writing a research paper in 24 hours is not as hard as it sound. In the next few pages, I will give you a clear outline on how to do so.

- Understand your assignment/syllabus and know exactly what the instructor wants as far as format and subject matter.

- Create a creative two part title and begin thinking about different angles you can take with the assignment.
- Library gathering sources (get this time down to 15 minutes).
- Highlight information in printed articles that will be used in the paper (1-2 hours).
- Use notecards or tabs to mark pages in books (1-2 hours).
- Transfer all quotes and passages from articles and books into one document on your computer (4-6 hours based on typing speed).
- Arrange information in an order that makes sense (1-2 hours).
- Make subtitles to direct the flow and shifts in information (1-2 hour)
- Expound on information and work on transitional sentences (2-3 hours).
- Tie everything together in a conclusion/ refine the body of your work (3-4 hours).
- Proofread several times (1-2 hour).

If followed loosely, this should take only 24 hours. If followed strictly, it can take much less time. If you take only 4 hours a day to work on your assignment, you will be done in less than a week. Knowing how quickly this task can be done takes the fear out of writing.

I strongly encourage each reader to practice these methods and put emphasis on creativity. Pushing the limits and taking chances that pay off will increase your confidence on future assignments. As stated before, if your instructor is strict on their particular format, follow it. As strict as they might be, the timeline outlined above can still be used.

In time, this will become second nature. Even if one step takes you several days, that is perfectly fine. Remember, most assignments are given at the beginning of the course and isn't expected until the end of the course. This gives you several weeks to study the information presented and think about creative ways to present your research. You now have key basic tools to excel; now make the transition to expert!

Afterword

Putting this book together has been a blessing and a labor of love. Creativity is a lost art that need to be resurrected. Once resurrected and embraced, the sky is the limit. The only limits are the ones you accept.

This book was short and to the point for a reason. My methods are so effective, I do not need to spend several pages of your time qualifying myself as a writer. If I was struggling in school or the workplace, I would want to know things I can use instantly to help improve my writing. This book introduced methods and examples.

Just because you're in school trying to meet graduation requirements, you don't have to limit your experience. Who says you cant go above and beyond for yourself? Who says you can't research topics you are passionate about and begin critiquing articles and blogging about new things you're working on? Who says you can master a thing before you get the actual college degree?

Now that you're on your way to writing research papers in 24 hours, make a future goal to do them in 12. Again, you don't have to limit yourself. To get the full effect and the opportunity to experience incredible speed, contact me for one on one tutoring. I can be reached on social media networks or the following email address:

privateresearchtutor@gmail.com

"It is never too late to educate yourself!"

About the author
Roney McIntyre, Jr.

Roney McIntyre, Jr. is a proud honors graduate of the New Orleans Parish public school system. Some of his achievements were being awarded the Semper Fidelis Award for Musical Excellence and the American Legion Certificate of School Award for Leadership. Roney was also awarded a certificate for leadership in the study of criminal justice upon graduating college. He continues to display leadership in his actions, words, and pursuit of happiness.

Other Publications by
Roney McIntyre, Jr.

I Wrote the Book of Love "Valentines edition" (2014)

I Wrote the Book of Love (2013)

The Price of Life: Breaking strongholds and Building self-esteem" (2008)

Printed in Great Britain
by Amazon